CHRISTMAS HITS FOR TWO

ISBN 978-1-4950-6922-2

HAL•LEONARD® CORPORATION

7777 W. BLUEMOUND RD. P.O. BOX 13819 MILWAUKEE, WI 53213

Visit Hal Leonard Online at
www.halleonard.com

CONTENTS

ALL I WANT FOR CHRISTMAS IS YOU

VIOLINS

Words and Music by MARIAH CAREY
and WALTER AFANASIEFF

BABY, IT'S COLD OUTSIDE
from the Motion Picture NEPTUNE'S DAUGHTER

By FRANK LOESSER

VIOLINS

THE CHRISTMAS SONG
(Chestnuts Roasting on an Open Fire)

VIOLINS

Music and Lyric by MEL TORMÉ
and ROBERT WELLS

THE CHRISTMAS WALTZ

VIOLINS

Words by SAMMY CAHN
Music by JULE STYNE

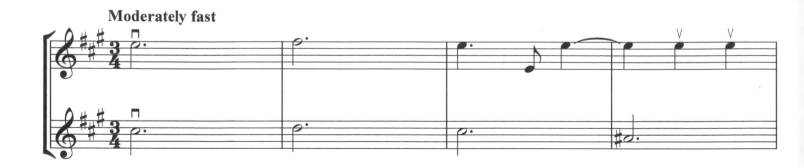

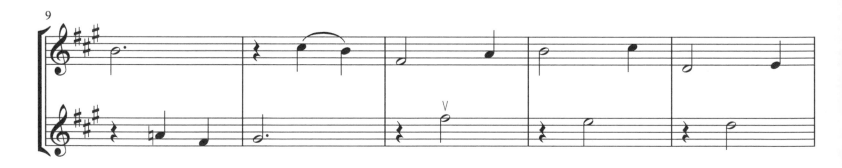

DO YOU HEAR WHAT I HEAR

VIOLINS

Words and Music by NOEL REGNEY
and GLORIA SHAYNE

DO YOU WANT TO BUILD A SNOWMAN?
from FROZEN

VIOLINS

Music and Lyrics by KRISTEN ANDERSON-LOPEZ
and ROBERT LOPEZ

FELIZ NAVIDAD

VIOLINS

Music and Lyrics by
JOSÉ FELICIANO

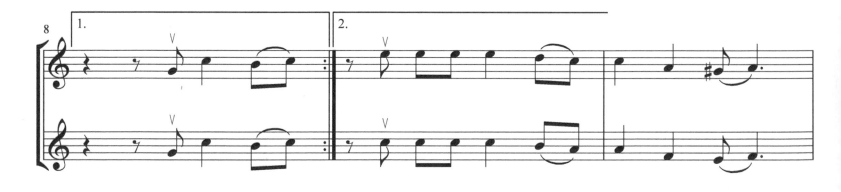

HAVE YOURSELF A MERRY LITTLE CHRISTMAS

from MEET ME IN ST. LOUIS

VIOLINS

Words and Music by HUGH MARTIN
and RALPH BLANE

HERE COMES SANTA CLAUS
(Right Down Santa Claus Lane)

VIOLINS

Words and Music by GENE AUTRY
and OAKLEY HALDEMAN

A HOLLY JOLLY CHRISTMAS

VIOLINS

Music and Lyrics by
JOHNNY MARKS

(There's No Place Like)
HOME FOR THE HOLIDAYS

VIOLINS

Words and Music by AL STILLMAN
and ROBERT ALLEN

Moderately fast

D.S. al Fine

I'LL BE HOME FOR CHRISTMAS

VIOLINS

Words and Music by KIM GANNON
and WALTER KENT

Moderately

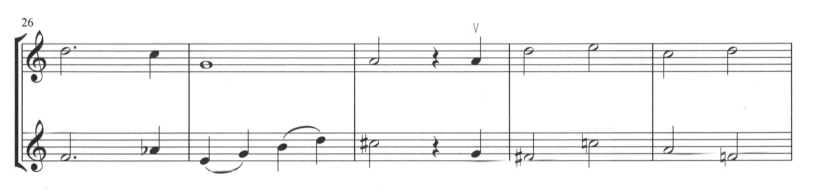

IT'S BEGINNING TO LOOK LIKE CHRISTMAS

VIOLINS

By MEREDITH WILLSON

LET IT SNOW! LET IT SNOW! LET IT SNOW!

VIOLINS

Words by SAMMY CAHN
Music by JULE STYNE

MARY, DID YOU KNOW?

VIOLINS

Words and Music by MARK LOWRY
and BUDDY GREENE

THE MOST WONDERFUL TIME OF THE YEAR

VIOLINS

Words and Music by EDDIE POLA
and GEORGE WYLE

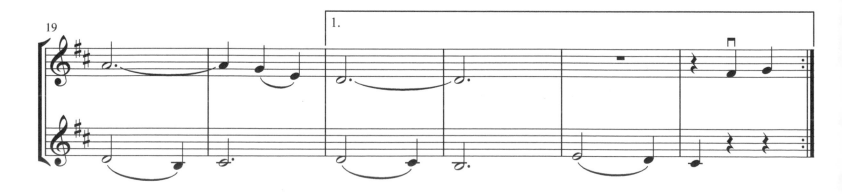

MY FAVORITE THINGS
from THE SOUND OF MUSIC

VIOLINS

Lyrics by OSCAR HAMMERSTEIN II
Music by RICHARD RODGERS

ROCKIN' AROUND THE CHRISTMAS TREE

VIOLINS

Music and Lyrics by
JOHNNY MARKS

RUDOLPH THE RED-NOSED REINDEER

VIOLINS

Music and Lyrics by
JOHNNY MARKS

SILVER BELLS
from the Paramount Picture THE LEMON DROP KID

VIOLINS

Words and Music by JAY LIVINGSTON
and RAY EVANS

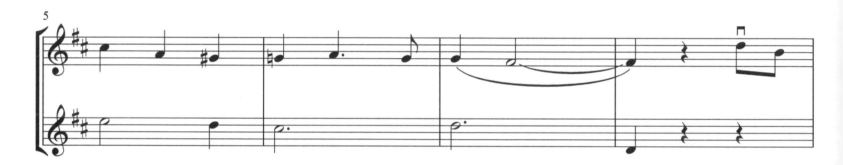

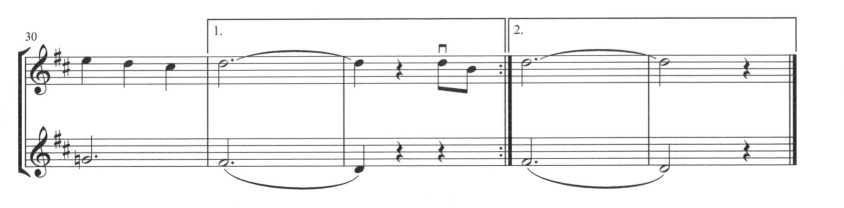

SOMEWHERE IN MY MEMORY
from the Twentieth Century Fox Motion Picture HOME ALONE

VIOLINS

Words by LESLIE BRICUSSE
Music by JOHN WILLIAMS

WHITE CHRISTMAS

from the Motion Picture Irving Berlin's HOLIDAY INN

VIOLINS

Words and Music by
IRVING BERLIN

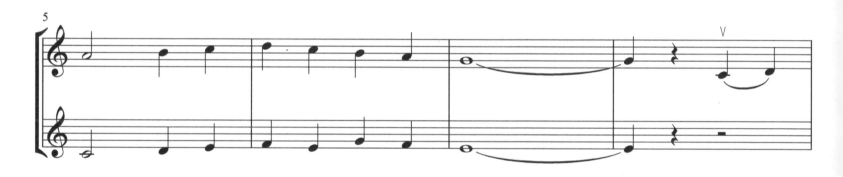

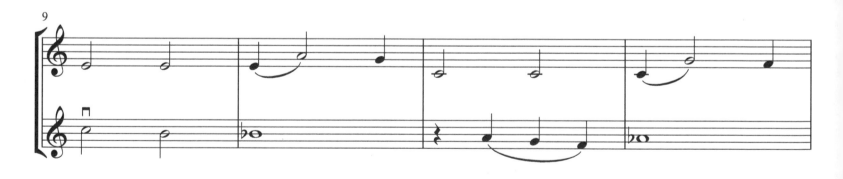

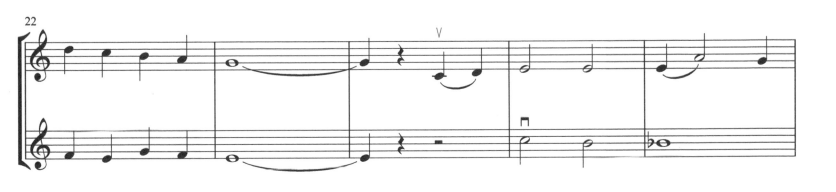

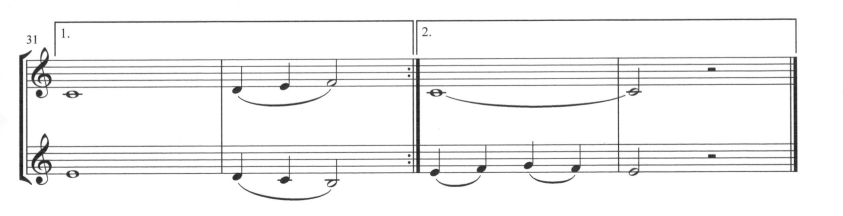

HAL•LEONARD INSTRUMENTAL PLAY-ALONG

Your favorite songs are arranged just for solo instrumentalists with this outstanding series. Each book includes great full-accompaniment play-along audio so you can sound just like a pro!

Check out **halleonard.com** for songlists and more titles!

12 Pop Hits
12 songs
00261790	Flute	00261795	Horn
00261791	Clarinet	00261796	Trombone
00261792	Alto Sax	00261797	Violin
00261793	Tenor Sax	00261798	Viola
00261794	Trumpet	00261799	Cello

The Very Best of Bach
15 selections
00225371	Flute	00225376	Horn
00225372	Clarinet	00225377	Trombone
00225373	Alto Sax	00225378	Violin
00225374	Tenor Sax	00225379	Viola
00225375	Trumpet	00225380	Cello

The Beatles
15 songs
00225330	Flute	00225335	Horn
00225331	Clarinet	00225336	Trombone
00225332	Alto Sax	00225337	Violin
00225333	Tenor Sax	00225338	Viola
00225334	Trumpet	00225339	Cello

Chart Hits
12 songs
00146207	Flute	00146212	Horn
00146208	Clarinet	00146213	Trombone
00146209	Alto Sax	00146214	Violin
00146210	Tenor Sax	00146211	Trumpet
00146216	Cello		

Christmas Songs
12 songs
00146855	Flute	00146863	Horn
00146858	Clarinet	00146864	Trombone
00146859	Alto Sax	00146866	Violin
00146860	Tenor Sax	00146867	Viola
00146862	Trumpet	00146868	Cello

Contemporary Broadway
15 songs
00298704	Flute	00298709	Horn
00298705	Clarinet	00298710	Trombone
00298706	Alto Sax	00298711	Violin
00298707	Tenor Sax	00298712	Viola
00298708	Trumpet	00298713	Cello

Disney Movie Hits
12 songs
00841420	Flute	00841424	Horn
00841687	Oboe	00841425	Trombone
00841421	Clarinet	00841426	Violin
00841422	Alto Sax	00841427	Viola
00841686	Tenor Sax	00841428	Cello
00841423	Trumpet		

Prices, contents, and availability subject to change without notice.

Disney characters and artwork ™ & © 2021 Disney

Disney Solos
12 songs
00841404	Flute	00841506	Oboe
00841406	Alto Sax	00841409	Trumpet
00841407	Horn	00841410	Violin
00841411	Viola	00841412	Cello
00841405	Clarinet/Tenor Sax		
00841408	Trombone/Baritone		
00841553	Mallet Percussion		

Dixieland Favorites
15 songs
00268756	Flute	0068759	Trumpet
00268757	Clarinet	00268760	Trombone
00268758	Alto Sax		

Billie Eilish
9 songs
00345648	Flute	00345653	Horn
00345649	Clarinet	00345654	Trombone
00345650	Alto Sax	00345655	Violin
00345651	Tenor Sax	00345656	Viola
00345652	Trumpet	00345657	Cello

Favorite Movie Themes
13 songs
00841166	Flute	00841168	Trumpet
00841167	Clarinet	00841170	Trombone
00841169	Alto Sax	00841296	Violin

Gospel Hymns
15 songs
00194648	Flute	00194654	Trombone
00194649	Clarinet	00194655	Violin
00194650	Alto Sax	00194656	Viola
00194651	Tenor Sax	00194657	Cello
00194652	Trumpet		

Great Classical Themes
15 songs
00292727	Flute	00292733	Horn
00292728	Clarinet	00292735	Trombone
00292729	Alto Sax	00292736	Violin
00292730	Tenor Sax	00292737	Viola
00292732	Trumpet	00292738	Cello

The Greatest Showman
8 songs
00277389	Flute	00277394	Horn
00277390	Clarinet	00277395	Trombone
00277391	Alto Sax	00277396	Violin
00277392	Tenor Sax	00277397	Viola
00277393	Trumpet	00277398	Cello

Irish Favorites
31 songs
00842489	Flute	00842495	Trombone
00842490	Clarinet	00842496	Violin
00842491	Alto Sax	00842497	Viola
00842493	Trumpet	00842498	Cello
00842494	Horn		

Michael Jackson
11 songs
00119495	Flute	00119499	Trumpet
00119496	Clarinet	00119501	Trombone
00119497	Alto Sax	00119503	Violin
00119498	Tenor Sax	00119502	Accomp.

Jazz & Blues
14 songs
00841438	Flute	00841441	Trumpet
00841439	Clarinet	00841443	Trombone
00841440	Alto Sax	00841444	Violin
00841442	Tenor Sax		

Jazz Classics
12 songs
00151812	Flute	00151816	Trumpet
00151813	Clarinet	00151818	Trombone
00151814	Alto Sax	00151819	Violin
00151815	Tenor Sax	00151821	Cello

Les Misérables
13 songs
00842292	Flute	00842297	Horn
00842293	Clarinet	00842298	Trombone
00842294	Alto Sax	00842299	Violin
00842295	Tenor Sax	00842300	Viola
00842296	Trumpet	00842301	Cello

Metallica
12 songs
02501327	Flute	02502454	Horn
02501339	Clarinet	02501329	Trombone
02501332	Alto Sax	02501334	Violin
02501333	Tenor Sax	02501335	Viola
02501330	Trumpet	02501338	Cello

Motown Classics
15 songs
00842572	Flute	00842576	Trumpet
00842573	Clarinet	00842578	Trombone
00842574	Alto Sax	00842579	Violin
00842575	Tenor Sax		

Pirates of the Caribbean
16 songs
00842183	Flute	00842188	Horn
00842184	Clarinet	00842189	Trombone
00842185	Alto Sax	00842190	Violin
00842186	Tenor Sax	00842191	Viola
00842187	Trumpet	00842192	Cello

Queen
17 songs
00285402	Flute	00285407	Horn
00285403	Clarinet	00285408	Trombone
00285404	Alto Sax	00285409	Violin
00285405	Tenor Sax	00285410	Viola
00285406	Trumpet	00285411	Cello

Simple Songs
14 songs
00249081	Flute	00249087	Horn
00249093	Oboe	00249089	Trombone
00249082	Clarinet	00249090	Violin
00249083	Alto Sax	00249091	Viola
00249084	Tenor Sax	00249092	Cello
00249086	Trumpet	00249094	Mallets

Superhero Themes
14 songs
00363195	Flute	00363200	Horn
00363196	Clarinet	00363201	Trombone
00363197	Alto Sax	00363202	Violin
00363198	Tenor Sax	00363203	Viola
00363199	Trumpet	00363204	Cello

Star Wars
16 songs
00350900	Flute	00350907	Horn
00350913	Oboe	00350908	Trombone
00350903	Clarinet	00350909	Violin
00350904	Alto Sax	00350910	Viola
00350905	Tenor Sax	00350911	Cello
00350906	Trumpet	00350914	Mallet

Taylor Swift
15 songs
00842532	Flute	00842537	Horn
00842533	Clarinet	00842538	Trombone
00842534	Alto Sax	00842539	Violin
00842535	Tenor Sax	00842540	Viola
00842536	Trumpet	00842541	Cello

Video Game Music
13 songs
00283877	Flute	00283883	Horn
00283878	Clarinet	00283884	Trombone
00283879	Alto Sax	00283885	Violin
00283880	Tenor Sax	00283886	Viola
00283882	Trumpet	00283887	Cello

Wicked
13 songs
00842236	Flute	00842241	Horn
00842237	Clarinet	00842242	Trombone
00842238	Alto Sax	00842243	Violin
00842239	Tenor Sax	00842244	Viola
00842240	Trumpet	00842245	Cello

HAL•LEONARD®